SHAPING THE DEBATE

Defining and Discussing
IMMIGRATION

Christy Mihaly

Rourke
Educational Media

A Division of
Carson
Dellosa
Education

rourkeeducationalmedia.com

ROURKE'S
SCHOOL to HOME
CONNECTIONS
BEFORE AND DURING READING ACTIVITIES

Before Reading: *Building Background Knowledge and Vocabulary*

Building background knowledge can help children process new information and build upon what they already know. Before reading a book, it is important to tap into what children already know about the topic. This will help them develop their vocabulary and increase their reading comprehension.

Questions and Activities to Build Background Knowledge:

1. Look at the front cover of the book and read the title. What do you think this book will be about?
2. What do you already know about this topic?
3. Take a book walk and skim the pages. Look at the table of contents, photographs, captions, and bold words. Did these text features give you any information or predictions about what you will read in this book?

Vocabulary: *Vocabulary Is Key to Reading Comprehension*

Use the following directions to prompt a conversation about each word.
- Read the vocabulary words.
- What comes to mind when you see each word?
- What do you think each word means?

Vocabulary Words:
- *authorization*
- *border*
- *colonies*
- *deport*
- *executive*
- *implementation*
- *opposition*
- *persecution*
- *sanctuary*
- *terrorism*
- *tolerance*
- *undocumented*

During Reading: *Reading for Meaning and Understanding*

To achieve deep comprehension of a book, children are encouraged to use close reading strategies. During reading, it is important to have children stop and make connections. These connections result in deeper analysis and understanding of a book.

Close Reading a Text

During reading, have children stop and talk about the following:
- Any confusing parts
- Any unknown words
- Text to text, text to self, text to world connections
- The main idea in each chapter or heading

Encourage children to use context clues to determine the meaning of any unknown words. These strategies will help children learn to analyze the text more thoroughly as they read.

When you are finished reading this book, turn to page 46 for **Text-Dependent Questions** and an **Extension Activity**.

TABLE OF CONTENTS

CHAPTER ONE

A CRISIS IN IMMIGRATION

In the spring of 2018, Americans learned that their government was separating thousands of children from their parents. People across the country were shocked to see images of youngsters—some less than two years old—crying within chain-link enclosures and sleeping on concrete floors under thin foil sheets.

The federal government was following a new "zero **tolerance**" policy. This meant it was treating all those entering the United States without legal permission as criminals. At the southwestern **border**, many families sought asylum—legal protection and permission to stay— fearing violence from gangs in their home countries. Previously, such families had been allowed to stay together in the U.S. while awaiting decisions on their asylum applications. Under the new policy, parents were arrested and sent to jail, while children were taken away and held elsewhere. Parents and children didn't know if they'd ever see one another again.

People seeking asylum start the process by turning themselves in at the U.S. border. They are then sent to immigration jail and later interviewed at an asylum office—part of the U.S. Citizenship and Immigration Services.

Seeking Asylum

To receive permission to remain in the U.S., asylum seekers must show that they fear abuse or oppression in their home countries due to race, religion, nationality, politics, or membership in a persecuted group. The United States approves only about 20 percent of asylum applications.

Many Americans protested the separations, shouting, "Families belong together!" Meanwhile, U.S. Attorney General Jeff Sessions defended the new policy. He said it would cause families to stay in their own countries rather than risk being separated. In June 2018, a court ordered the government to reunify the parents and children. President Donald Trump then declared the government would work to hold families in detention together.

In June 2018, protesters across the United States held hundreds of demonstrations calling for an end to family separations.

These events were part of a larger ongoing immigration debate. Some Americans are concerned that too many immigrants have moved in and that immigration harms the country. Others point out that immigrants contribute to the United States in important ways. Many agree that the nation's laws controlling immigration should be overhauled. It's a complex issue with a complicated history and no easy answers.

People found creative ways to express their views about President Trump and immigration policies.

How Many?

The United States is home to more immigrants than any other country. In 2017, 44.5 million people living in the U.S.—almost 14 percent—were born elsewhere. In total, the combination of immigrants plus their American-born children makes up 27 percent of the population.

Demonstrators marched for changes in immigration laws. Some wanted to make it easier to gain citizenship; others wanted to reduce immigration.

CHAPTER TWO

THE HISTORY OF UNITED STATES IMMIGRATION

The United States was built upon immigration. From the 16th through the 18th centuries, many thousands of settlers from England, Spain, and elsewhere in Europe sought opportunities in North American **colonies**. They were joined by convicted criminals and prison inmates who were often transported involuntarily. And millions of men, women, and children were enslaved and shipped from Africa.

Early European immigrants to the U.S. could not have survived without the assistance of American Indians.

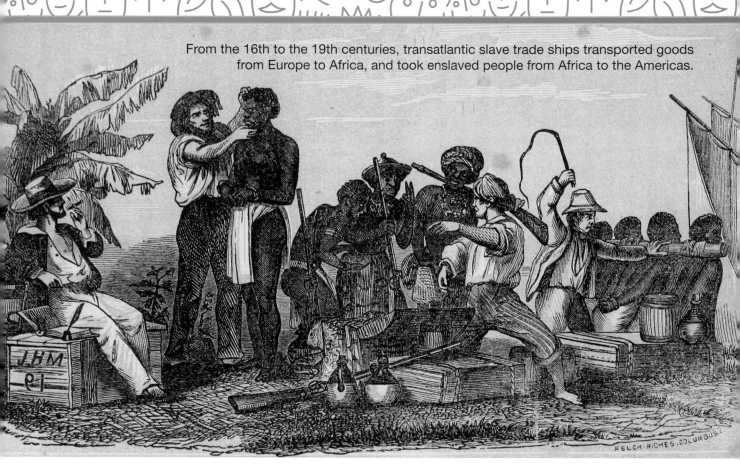

From the 16th to the 19th centuries, transatlantic slave trade ships transported goods from Europe to Africa, and took enslaved people from Africa to the Americas.

Original Inhabitants

Scientists believe the original human inhabitants of North America migrated from Asia across a prehistoric land bridge. These were the ancestors of the American Indians who lived all across the continent when Europeans arrived.

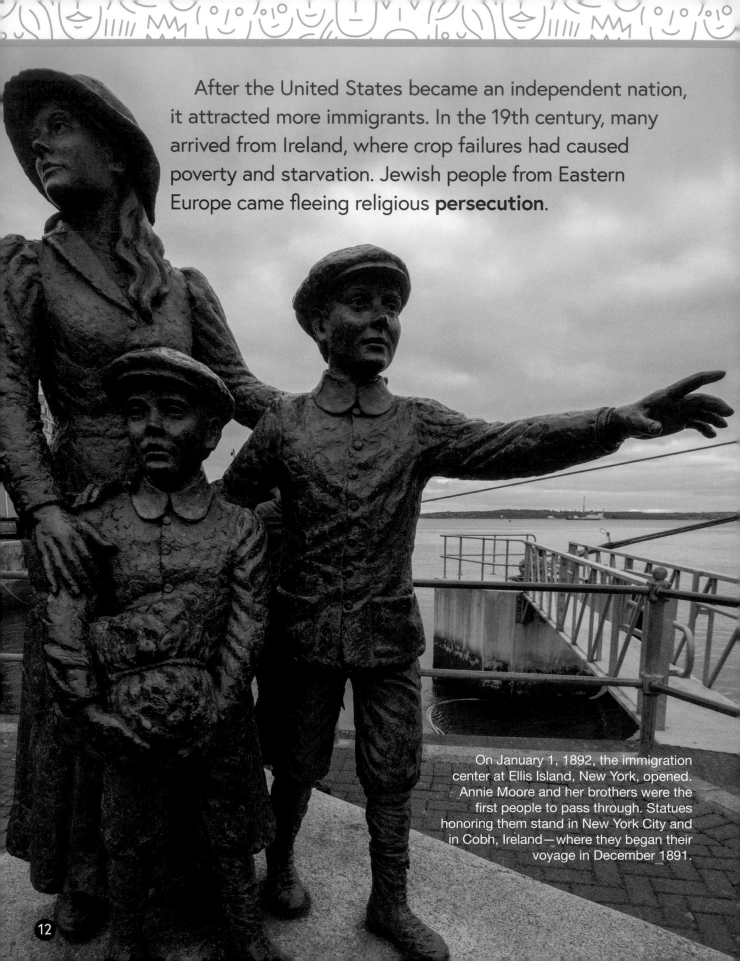

After the United States became an independent nation, it attracted more immigrants. In the 19th century, many arrived from Ireland, where crop failures had caused poverty and starvation. Jewish people from Eastern Europe came fleeing religious **persecution**.

On January 1, 1892, the immigration center at Ellis Island, New York, opened. Annie Moore and her brothers were the first people to pass through. Statues honoring them stand in New York City and in Cobh, Ireland—where they began their voyage in December 1891.

As news of the California Gold Rush spread, many thousands of Chinese immigrants crossed the Pacific Ocean to mine for gold, to work in factories and on farms, and to build new railroads.

This late 1800s cartoon shows Uncle Sam, representing the U.S., kicking Chinese workers out of the country.

Some citizens complained that the newcomers weren't "real Americans," and called for stricter limitations on immigration. Tensions arose around the large number of Chinese immigrants in particular. In 1882, Congress enacted the Chinese Exclusion Act, banning immigration by workers from China.

Immigrants arrive in the U.S.

By 1890, immigrants made up almost 15 percent of the U.S. population. In the 1920s, Congress imposed a quota system. This capped the number of immigration visas, or permits to enter, given to people from each country. The Immigration Act of 1924 allocated 69 percent of visas to people from the United Kingdom, Germany, and Ireland. It barred all immigrants from Asia.

President Calvin Coolidge signed the 1924 immigration law against the objections of Japan, which considered the new policy a national humiliation.

President Lyndon Johnson promoted the 1965 immigration reform, which he said would "strengthen us in a hundred unseen ways." He signed the new law at the foot of the Statue of Liberty.

In 1965, Congress ended this system of national quotas. Under the Immigration and Nationality Act of 1965, eligibility to immigrate would depend on job skills and family relationships with citizens rather than on nationality or race. Subsequently, immigration from non-European countries increased.

The U.S. Immigration and Naturalization Service (INS) enforced immigration laws from 1933 until a government reorganization in 2003.

CHAPTER THREE

TWENTY-FIRST CENTURY REGULATION OF IMMIGRATION

After attacks on the U.S. by foreign-born al-Qaeda terrorists on September 11, 2001, Congress created the Department of Homeland Security (DHS). DHS is charged with protecting the U.S. from **terrorism**, controlling immigration, and guarding the nation's borders.

Customs and Border Protection officers guard the nation's borders, such as this section of fence on the border with Mexico.

The Department of Homeland Security, created in 2002, employs more than 240,000 people.

DHS enforces federal immigration laws through three main branches. One, U.S. Citizenship and Immigration Services (USCIS), oversees legal immigration. It reviews petitions for lawful permanent residency, issues green cards to legal residents, and processes citizenship applications.

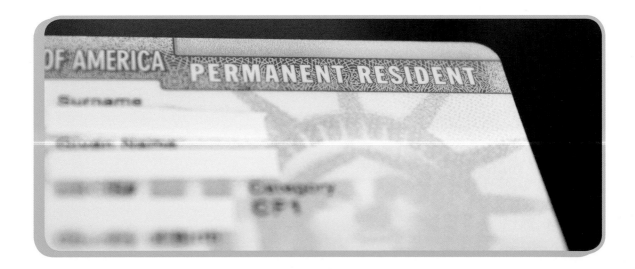

Legal Immigration

People seeking green cards, or permission for permanent residency, must meet numerous requirements. First, they usually need a sponsor to petition USCIS for an immigrant visa. Both USCIS and a U.S. Embassy must approve this visa, which allows legal entry to the U.S. USCIS issues the green card after entry.

Border agents police the U.S.-Mexico border on ATVs.

A second DHS agency, Immigration and Customs Enforcement (ICE), investigates **undocumented** immigrants. ICE can initiate deportation, returning immigrants to their home countries. A third agency, U.S. Customs and Border Protection (CBP), keeps the borders secure. CBP works to prevent terrorists, criminals, illegal drugs, and prohibited weapons from entering the U.S.

Homeland Security officers stand guard.

When immigration cases go to court—as when a person seeks asylum or when the government moves to **deport** someone—they are heard in special immigration courts. These courts are part of the U.S. Department of Justice, which is headed by the Attorney General of the United States.

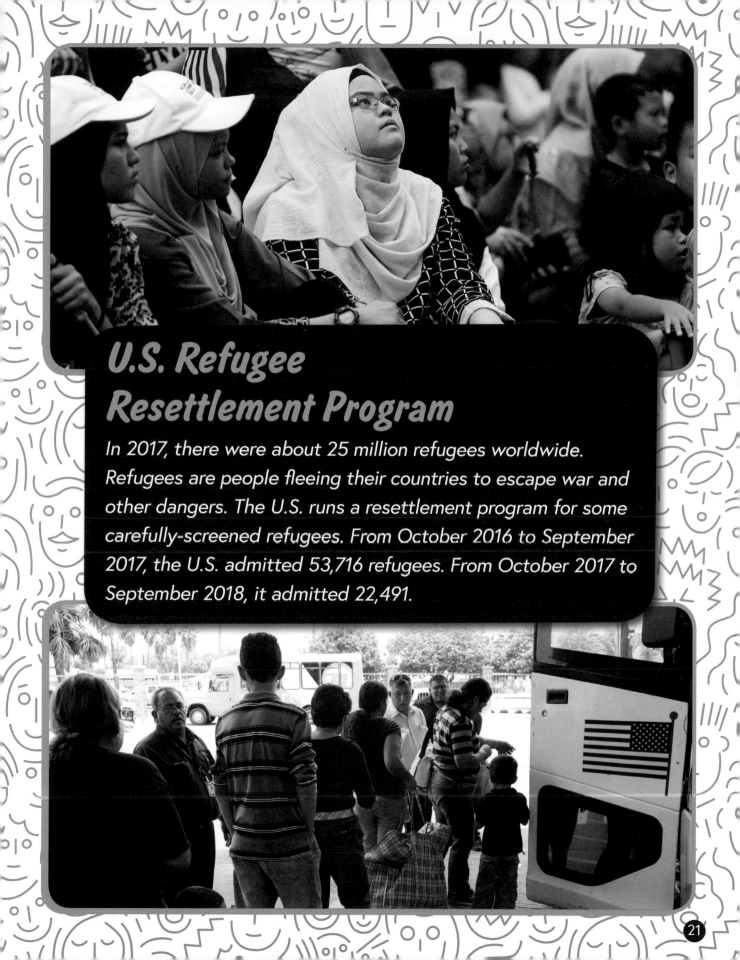

U.S. Refugee Resettlement Program

In 2017, there were about 25 million refugees worldwide. Refugees are people fleeing their countries to escape war and other dangers. The U.S. runs a resettlement program for some carefully-screened refugees. From October 2016 to September 2017, the U.S. admitted 53,716 refugees. From October 2017 to September 2018, it admitted 22,491.

CHAPTER FOUR

THE IMPACTS OF IMMIGRATION

Immigrants have shaped the United States throughout its history. Alexander Hamilton, a founder of the nation, was born on the Caribbean island of Nevis. Sergey Brin, from Russia, founded Google. American culture—music, movies, food, books, and art—as well as science and business, all benefit from the talents of immigrants.

Alexander Hamilton
1757 - 1804

Slovenian-born first lady Melania Trump became a U.S. citizen in 2006.

Albert Einstein
1879–1955

Physicist Albert Einstein had already won a Nobel Prize in physics when he fled Nazi Germany in 1933. He moved to Princeton, New Jersey, where he continued his work and also organized a refugee-aid group to help others escape the Nazis in Europe.

Notable Immigrants to the U.S.

Examples of well-known immigrants include Chimamanda Ngozi Adichie (author, Nigeria); Madeleine Albright (Secretary of State, Czechoslovakia); Albert Einstein (scientist, Germany); Gloria Estefan (singer, Cuba); Dikembe Mutombo (basketball star, Democratic Republic of the Congo); I.M. Pei (architect, China); Carlos Santana (musician, Mexico); Arnold Schwarzenegger (California governor, Austria); and Melania Trump (first lady, Slovenia).

In 2017, Hispanic or Latino people made up 18.1 percent of the U.S. population. Blacks made up 13.4 percent and people of Asian descent 5.8 percent, while 2.7 percent identified as two or more races. Whites who do not identify as Hispanic or Latino made up 60.7 percent of the population. The U.S. Census Bureau estimates that this group will become a minority of the population by 2045.

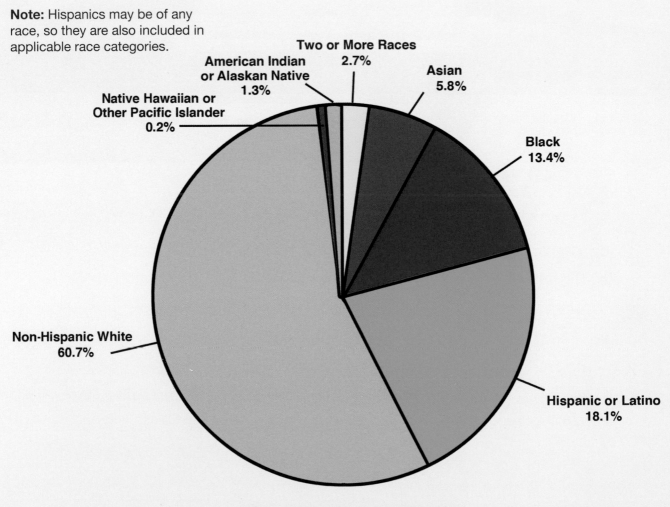

Note: Hispanics may be of any race, so they are also included in applicable race categories.

Two or More Races 2.7%

American Indian or Alaskan Native 1.3%

Native Hawaiian or Other Pacific Islander 0.2%

Asian 5.8%

Black 13.4%

Non-Hispanic White 60.7%

Hispanic or Latino 18.1%

2017 U.S. Census Bureau

Many Americans opposed President Barack Obama's efforts to extend amnesty, or relief from deportation, to undocumented immigrants.

Such diversity brings both cultural richness and the potential for conflict. For example, some Americans like to hear people in their communities speaking different languages. Others, though, argue that too many immigrants don't learn English. Opinions differ, but the fact is that while millions in the U.S. speak languages other than English, the majority of those also speak at least some English. Many immigrants must learn English in order to succeed.

Some people say immigrants take jobs away from non-immigrant workers. Further, when many low-income immigrants move into a community, existing residents may face additional costs. The newcomers use public services such as schools, which can cause local taxes to rise.

But most expert research finds that immigration provides important economic advantages to the nation. Immigrants spend money on homes, food, and other goods, and they pay taxes. Many start new businesses, generating more jobs. Immigration also helps keep the population younger, which helps the economy.

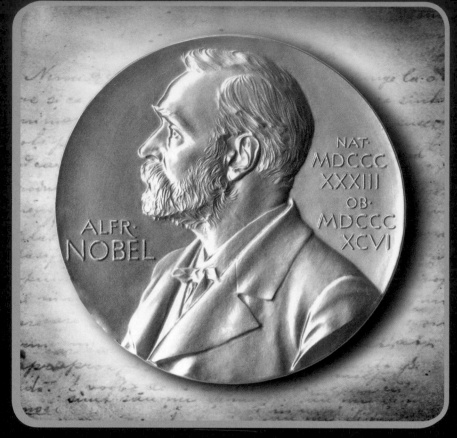

The Nobel Prize is an international honor awarded for outstanding contributions and achievements in the fields of physics, chemistry, physiology or medicine, economics, literature, and peace.

Dr. Elizabeth H. Blackburn of the University of California, San Francisco, is a Nobel Prize winner. She immigrated to the U.S. in the 1970s.

Nobel Winners

Between 2000 and 2017, 33 out of the 85 American winners of the Nobel Prize in chemistry, medicine, and physics were immigrants. That's 39 percent. Immigrants develop and patent new inventions at high rates, too.

Families seeking ayslum turn themselves over to immigration authorities at the border. In 2018, thousands of migrants fleeing Central America banded together for safety in "caravans" to make the long journey to the United States.

Some fear that immigrants bring crime. However, statistics show that immigrants to the U.S. commit crimes at lower rates than non-immigrants. Violent crime rates have fallen as immigrant populations have increased. Many undocumented immigrants do break immigration laws by entering the U.S. Yet, as White House Chief of Staff John Kelly stated in May 2018, "The vast majority of the people that move illegally into the United States are not bad people. They're not criminals."

CHAPTER FIVE

PROTECTING THE BORDERS

Because the September 11 terrorists were foreign-born Muslims, particular suspicion subsequently fell upon Muslim immigrants. In his presidential campaign, Donald Trump promised to keep Muslims out. In January 2017, President Trump signed an **executive** order which temporarily barred people from seven predominantly Muslim nations from entering the U.S.

President Trump signs the order.

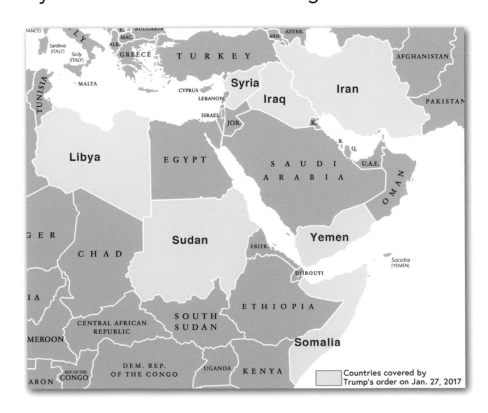

Countries covered by Trump's order on Jan. 27, 2017

In the resulting confusion, incoming travelers from the listed countries, including students heading to school and family members meeting loved ones, were stranded in airports or immediately sent home. Civil rights groups challenged the measure, arguing it improperly discriminated against one religion. Courts quickly blocked its enforcement.

In the days after Trump signed the so-called Muslim ban, thousands of people protested. Hundreds of volunteer lawyers gathered in airports to help travelers—many of them green card holders—who were told they could not enter the country.

President Trump then signed a revised order, exempting people with green cards and visas and removing Iraq from the list. In September 2017, a third order made changes that included adding North Korea and Venezuela to the list and removing Sudan. In June 2018, the U.S. Supreme Court upheld the third order on a 5-4 vote. The majority found it a valid exercise of the president's power to secure the borders.

The U.S. Supreme Court, shown in June 2017, has nine members. They are, standing: Justices Kagan, Alito, Sotomayor, and Gorsuch; seated: Justices Ginsburg and Kennedy (retired 2018), Chief Justice Roberts, Justices Thomas and Breyer.

In late 2017, eight models, or prototypes, of a possible border wall were completed in southern California. Some were up to 30 feet (9 meters) tall, about twice the height of existing sections of fence and wall.

The government said certain people from the listed countries (Iran, Libya, North Korea, Somalia, Syria, Venezuela, and Yemen) could apply for special permission to enter. Legal challenges to the **implementation** of the policy continued, as did the debate over how best to protect Americans against terrorism.

The Trump administration focused on stopping people from crossing the U.S.-Mexico border. In his campaign, Trump promised to build "a big, beautiful wall" along the southern border. He said Mexico would pay for it.

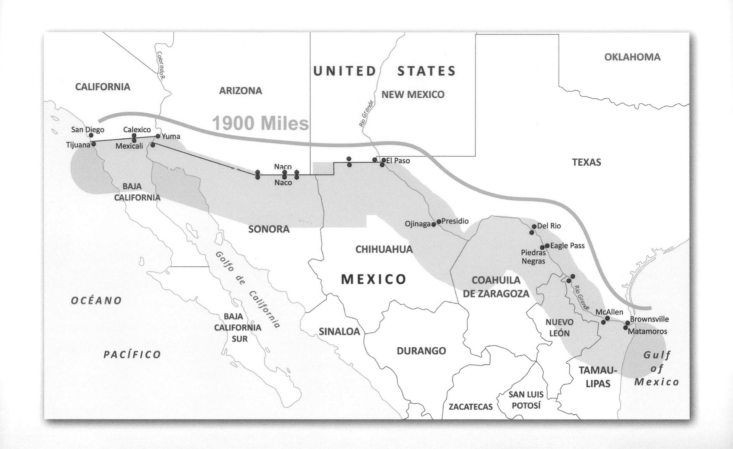

While many applauded Trump's proposal, the wall also faced extensive **opposition**. In addition to groups advocating for immigrants' rights, numerous landowners, businesses, and local governments along the border argued that a wall would harm their interests by blocking travel.

Border Dispute

The U.S.-Mexico border is about 1,900 miles (3,058 kilometers) long. About 75 miles (121 kilometers) cross the lands of the Tohono O'odham Nation. Tohono O'odham people live on both sides of the border and regularly cross it for business, school, medical treatment, and religious observances. They've resisted a wall.

El Paso, Texas, is located on the Rio Grande River. A bridge joins the city to Cuidad Juárez, Mexico.

The Mexican gray wolf, or "el lobo," was exterminated in the United States in the 1970s, and reintroduced into Arizona in 1998. Its population is recovering, but it remains endangered.

Walling the Desert

Environmentalists point out that a border wall cutting across the desert would damage fragile desert ecosystems, cut off animal migration routes, and threaten endangered species. Groups including the Sierra Club and Defenders of Wildlife have brought legal challenges to the proposed wall.

Early estimates projected that a border wall could cost up to 25 billion dollars—and Mexico declined to pay. Many in the U.S. argued this money would be better spent on other security measures. Congress was not eager to pass legislation to fund the wall. Despite general agreement that the U.S. should protect its borders, consensus on the specifics remained elusive.

"These aren't people. These are animals," President Trump said about some migrants seeking entry to the United States.

United States Capitol Building, home of the U.S. Congress

CHAPTER SIX

ADDRESSING ILLEGAL IMMIGRATION

There are about 11 million undocumented immigrants in the United States. They either entered without **authorization**, or they stayed after their temporary permission, such as a student visa, expired. Most of them work. Many have lived in the country for decades. Some arrived as children and know no other home.

U.S. Port of Entry
Peace Arch · Blaine, Washington

Some U.S. farms employ workers from abroad under a special visa program for temporary agricultural jobs.

Undocumented Farm Workers

About half of U.S. farm workers are undocumented immigrants. Farmers rely on immigrants to work long hours harvesting crops, milking cows, and doing difficult, dangerous tasks that most U.S. citizens don't want to do. Without these workers, thousands of farms would close, and Americans' food prices would be higher.

In California, the nation's top agricultural producer, farmers have trouble finding enough workers, and at times must leave crops unharvested. A majority of California farmworkers are immigrants; many are undocumented.

Polls show a majority of Americans support a path to citizenship for DREAMers.

Undocumented immigrants live in the shadows. For them, a traffic stop for driving with a broken headlight could result in being deported. The majority of undocumented immigrants are ineligible for government benefits, including Social Security benefits. In most states, they can't get driver's licenses. Most undocumented immigrants have no way to obtain legal status.

The DREAM (Development, Relief, and Education for Alien Minors) Act, introduced in Congress in 2001, was intended to provide a path to citizenship for some who arrived illegally as children. Congress has voted on the bill numerous times, but not passed it.

In 2012, President Obama announced that his administration would stop deporting certain undocumented immigrants. Under the Deferred Action for Childhood Arrivals (DACA) program, people who arrived before age 16 and met other standards could apply for temporary relief from deportation. But DACA did not provide a path to citizenship for these immigrants, the so-called "DREAMers."

Sanctuary Cities, Counties, and States

*Local police, when making arrests, send suspects' fingerprints to ICE. Then, ICE often asks police to hold undocumented immigrants for deportation. In hundreds of **sanctuary** cities and counties, however, police refuse. Sanctuary jurisdictions want to encourage immigrants to trust police. The Trump administration sued California over its sanctuary laws.*

In a July 2018 ruling, a federal judge refused to block California's "sanctuary state" law. The state had the power, the ruling said, to refuse to help enforce immigration laws, and to leave that enforcement to the U.S. government.

The DACA program enabled about 800,000 DREAMers to get driver's licenses and work permits, earn money, and further their education without fear of deportation. Economic analyses found that the impact of bringing

DREAMers into the legal economy—earning and spending more money—was positive for the country.

However, many opposed DACA. In 2017, the Trump administration opted to terminate the program. The termination was challenged in the courts. As the nation continued its ongoing discussion about reforming immigration laws, the fate of the DREAMers and other undocumented immigrants remained uncertain.

PRACTICE PREPARING FOR A DEBATE

People explain issues and solve problems through discussion. Debates are formal discussions about an issue. Debate participants present facts they have gathered from reliable sources. They present this information as they try to convince listeners that their opinions about an issue are correct.

Supplies

- paper
- pencil
- books on your topic and/or internet access

Directions:

1. Decide the topic you will research.

2. Write a question that will shape your debate. Example: Should religion be taught in public schools?

3. Write your proposition or opposition statement. Proposition example: Religion should be taught in public schools. Opposition example: Religion should not be taught in public schools.

4. Research your topic using a variety of sources. Make a list of the facts you find and note the source of each fact next to it.

5. Practice presenting your argument.

6. Flip the script! Follow steps 1 – 5 again, this time preparing with facts that support the other side.

Bonus: Form a debate club with your friends. Assign a new topic regularly. Give each person equal time to present their arguments.

Glossary

authorization (aw-thuh-ruh-ZAY-shuhn): official or legal approval or permission

border (BOR-dur): a dividing line between two countries, states, or regions

colonies (KAH-luh-neez): territories controlled by a distant nation and settled by people from that nation

deport (di-PORT): force to leave a country

executive (ig-ZEK-yuh-tiv): part of the branch of government that enforces the laws of the United States or a state

implementation (im-pluh-muhn-TAY-shuhn): the process of carrying out a decision or plan

opposition (ah-puh-ZISH-uhn): resistance or objection

persecution (pur-suh-KYOO-shuhn): cruel or harmful treatment or abuse of people, especially because of their race, religion, or political beliefs

sanctuary (SANGK-choo-air-ee): a safe place or a place that provides shelter or protection

terrorism (TER-uh-riz-uhm): unlawful and politically motivated use of violence to hurt and frighten people

tolerance (TAH-lur-uhns): willingness to allow something that one disagrees with

undocumented (uhn-DAHK-yuh-muhn-tid): lacking appropriate or required legal papers or permissions

Index

Text-Dependent Questions

1. What are some reasons that people have immigrated to the United States?

2. How does the Department of Homeland Security regulate immigration?

3. How has immigration affected the United States?

4. What are some ways President Trump used his presidential power to limit immigration?

5. How did DACA affect undocumented immigrants?

Extension Activity

Create a family tree showing where your grandparents were born. Can you track down where all of your great-grandparents came from? How about great-great-grandparents? Select an ancestor or family member who immigrated to America and dig into his or her story. How, when, and why did this person immigrate? Was he or she alone or with family? What was his or her first language? Did your family member become a U.S. citizen? Summarize this information on your family tree.

Bibliography

Agresti, James D., "Immigration Facts." Just Facts, last modified Dec. 14, 2018. www.justfacts.com/immigration.asp.

American Immigration Council website, https://www.americanimmigrationcouncil.org/. Accessed Dec. 17, 2018.

Barbash, Fred and Allyson Chiu, "Settlement Reached in Family Separation Cases." Washington Post, Sept. 13. 2018.

CNN Library, "Immigration Statistics Fast Facts," last modified Dec. 4, 2018. https://www.cnn.com/2013/11/06/us/immigration-statistics-fast-facts/index.html.

Center for American Progress, "The Facts on Immigration Today: 2017 Edition." https://www.americanprogress.org/issues/immigration/reports/2017/04/20/430736/facts-immigration-today-2017-edition/.

Center for Immigration Studies website. https://cis.org/. Accessed Dec. 17, 2018.

Dudley, Mary Jo, "These U.S. Industries Can't Work Without Illegal Immigrants," CBSNews/Moneywatch, June 25, 2018.

Lopez, Gustavo, Kristen Bialik and Jynnah Radford, "Key Findings About U.S. Immigrants," Pew Research Center/Fact Tank, Nov. 30, 2018. http://www.pewresearch.org/fact-tank/2018/09/14/key-findings-about-u-s-immigrants/.

Pitt, Andrew and Ian Goldin, Migration and the Economy: Economic Realities, Social Impacts, and Political Choices. Citi-Oxford Martin School-Global Perspectives and Solutions, September 2018. https://ir.citi.com/FBbeXUKehK94DM2ktog5Yjj4Eh9MKmUH34Poe/ZhEFhORbQvjK8I1BVlhg%2BCNS4WRzN1yW9UoM%3D

Robertson, Lori, Factcheck.org, "Illegal immigration: Separating the Facts from Fiction." USA Today, June 30, 2018.

Tavernise, Sabrina, "U.S. Has Highest Share of Foreign-Born Since 1910, With More Coming From Asia." New York Times, Sept. 13, 2018.

U.S. Census Bureau, "Quick Facts: United States." https://www.census.gov/quickfacts/fact/table/US/PST045217. Accessed Dec.17, 2018.

U.S. Department of State, Bureau of Population, Refugees, and Migration, Refugee Processing Center, "Admissions and Arrivals" (data), http://www.wrapsnet.org/admissions-and-arrivals/. Accessed December 17, 2018.

University of Pennsylvania, Wharton School, "Budget Model: The Effects of Immigration on the United States' Economy." June 27, 2016. http://budgetmodel.wharton.upenn.edu/issues/2016/1/27/the-effects-of-immigration-on-the-united-states-economy.

Zong, Jie, Jeanne Batalova, and Jeffrey Hallock, "Frequently Requested Statistics on Immigrants and Immigration in the United States." Migration Policy Institute, Feb. 8, 2018. https://www.migrationpolicy.org/article/frequently-requested-statistics-immigrants-and-immigration-united-states.

About the Author

Christy Mihaly writes nonfiction books, articles, poetry, and stories for young readers. She earned degrees in policy studies and law, and worked as an attorney for more than 20 years before becoming an author. Christy's ancestors and family members immigrated to the United States from throughout Europe as well as South America. She works in rural Vermont under the supervision of her dog and cat. Visit her at www.christymihaly.com.

www.rourkeeducationalmedia.com

PHOTO CREDITS: Cover; drawings of faces By topform | Shutterstock.com, photo By Prazis Images | Shutterstock.com; Pg.4-5: shutterstock.com | Gregory Dean, shutterstock.com | Suzanne Tucker, Pg.6-7: istock.com | sweetbabeejay, Editorial Shutterstock.com | Richard Thornton. Pg.8-9: istock.com | vichinterlang, istock.com|FireAtDusk. Pg.10-11: "Unknown" Public Domain Pg.12-13: istock.com | Maria_Janus. Pg.14-15: Shutterstock.com | Joseph Sohm, "Unknow" Public Domain. Pg.16-17: shutterstock.com | Mark Van Scyoc, shutterstock.com | Sherry V Smith, istock.com | DJMcCoy, shutterstock.com | Nuangthong. Pg.18-19: shutterstock.com | Evgenia Parajanian, Shutterstock.com | Eric Crudup, DHS/Border Patrol. Pg.20-21: stock.com | Wavebreakmedia, Editorial shutterstock.com | Nik Mazda Photography. Pg.22-23: istock.com | Prykhodov, Orren Jack Turner/PD, Editorial Shutterstock.com | mark reinstein. Pg.24-25: s.stratford, Shutterstock.com | Syda Productions, shutterstock.com | a katz. Pg.26-27: Editorial Shutterstock.com | Joseph Sohm, shutterstock.com | travelview. Pg.28-29: shutterstock.com | Paramonov Alexander, Conrad Erb/Science History Institute-CCA Share Alike 3.0 Unported, shutterstock.com | vichinterlang, DHS. Pg.30-31: istock.com | PeterHermesFurian, shutterstock.com | arindambanerjee. Pg.32-33: istock.com | PeterHermesFurian, istock.com | Greg Bulla. Pg.34-35: shutterstock.com | PhotoTrippingAmerica, shutterstock.com | Frontpage, shutterstock.com | Rainer Lesniewski. Pg.36-37: shutterstock.com | Nagel Photography, istock.com | 46travels, shutterstock.com | ANUJAK JAIMOO, shutterstock.com | Evan El-Amin. Pg.38-39: Shutterstock.com | aniel Avram, istock.com | vichinterlang, istock.com | rightdx. Pg.40-41: istock.com | DMEPhotography, istock.com | deberarr, istock.com | BackyardProduction, shutterstock.com | Christopher Penler. Pg.42-43: shutterstock.com | van El-Amin, ICE/DHLS, istock.com | miroslav_1, shutterstock.com | hrisdorney. Pg.44-45: istock.com | rrodrickbeiler, shutterstock.com | 1000 Words, shutterstock.com | Diego G Diaz.

Edited by: Kim Thompson
Produced by Blue Door Education for Rourke Educational Media. Cover and interior design by: Jennifer Dydyk

Library of Congress PCN Data

Defining and Discussing Immigration / Christy Mihaly
(Shaping the Debate)
ISBN 978-1-73161-471-1 (hard cover)
ISBN 978-1-73161-278-6 (soft cover)
ISBN 978-1-73161-576-3 (e-Book)
ISBN 978-1-73161-681-4 (e-Pub)
Library of Congress Control Number: 2019932388

Rourke Educational Media
Printed in the United States of America,
North Mankato, Minnesota